Sins of the Father

A Play

Leo Smith

A Samuel French Acting Edition

SAMUELFRENCH-LONDON.CO.UK
SAMUELFRENCH.COM

Copyright © 1992 by Leo Smith
All Rights Reserved

SINS OF THE FATHER is fully protected under the copyright laws of the British Commonwealth, including Canada, the United States of America, and all other countries of the Copyright Union. All rights, including professional and amateur stage productions, recitation, lecturing, public reading, motion picture, radio broadcasting, television and the rights of translation into foreign languages are strictly reserved.

ISBN 978-0-573-12253-8

www.samuelfrench-london.co.uk

www.samuelfrench.com

FOR AMATEUR PRODUCTION ENQUIRIES

UNITED KINGDOM AND WORLD
EXCLUDING NORTH AMERICA
plays@SamuelFrench-London.co.uk
020 7255 4302/01

Each title is subject to availability from Samuel French,
depending upon country of performance.

CAUTION: Professional and amateur producers are hereby warned that *SINS OF THE FATHER* is subject to a licensing fee. Publication of this play does not imply availability for performance. Both amateurs and professionals considering a production are strongly advised to apply to the appropriate agent before starting rehearsals, advertising, or booking a theatre. A licensing fee must be paid whether the title is presented for charity or gain and whether or not admission is charged.

The professional rights in this play are controlled by Samuel French Ltd, 52 Fitzroy Street, London, W1T 5JR.

No one shall make any changes in this title for the purpose of production. No part of this book may be reproduced, stored in a retrieval system, or transmitted in any form, by any means, now known or yet to be invented, including mechanical, electronic, photocopying, recording, videotaping, or otherwise, without the prior written permission of the publisher. No one shall upload this title, or part of this title, to any social media websites.

The right of Leo Smith to be identified as author of this work has been asserted by him in accordance with Section 77 of the Copyright, Designs and Patents Act 1988

CHARACTERS

Kevin Hargreaves
Frances Hargreaves
Kitty

The characters are not to be defined by age. The only constraints being that they should be old enough to have had the children as indicated by their ages

The action of the play takes place in two combined bedrooms. The first we see is that of Kitty; the second, indicated by a lighting change, that of Kevin and Frances Hargreaves

Time — the present, the past, the future

SINS OF THE FATHER

First performed by the Phoenix Theatre Company at the Southgate One Act Drama Festival in March 1991 with the following cast of characters:

Kevin Hargreaves	Tony Randall
Kitty	Linda Chandler
Frances Hargreaves	Hilary Bull

The play was directed by Leo Smith

PRODUCTION NOTE

Colours should be used to identify the two bedrooms. In the first production the bed linen was split to indicate the two areas. The flats used were painted to co-ordinate with the overall effect. Lighting was used effectively to define which acting area was in use for each scene. Strobe/chase lighting is suggested for the final scene.

SINS OF THE FATHER

Scene 1

As the Curtain *opens Kevin Hargreaves is lying on the double bed looking pleased with himself. Kitty is making up at a vanity unit* L. *She is smoking. She smokes throughout the play in a nasty, disgusting manner. Kevin, although a non-smoker, does not seem to mind this*

A few moments pass

Kitty It's time. (*She throws him a look*)

Pause

Kevin sighs deeply

Oh, do come on, Kevin. Stop contemplating your navel and start thinking about what you promised to do tonight.
Kevin All right. All right. I was just enjoying a bit of a post-coital relax, that's all. The calm before the storm, you know.
Kitty Not getting cold feet are you?

Pause

Kevin It's not exactly going to be easy, is it. I mean it's not every night you come home in the early hours and say, "Hello, dear. Yes, I did have a nice day at the office. Oh, and by the way, I've had a lovely time tonight screwing my mistress and I've decided to leave you."
Kitty I would hope you're going to be a little more subtle than that, dear.
Kevin (*snorting*) You don't really think I could be as crude or as cruel as that, do you?
Kitty I don't know. You've obviously got to be cruel at some stage.

Your wife doesn't even suspect you've been having an affair for the past two years. Or so you tell me.

Kevin No, she doesn't know. She's too busy looking after the kids. And when she's not doing that she's too tired to notice anything else. Besides, she trusts me.

Kitty Lucky you. I wouldn't trust you. I wouldn't trust the Archangel Gabriel. So. What are you going to tell her?

Kevin Poor Kitty. Had a rough time have we; in the past?

Kitty Look, Kevin, you leave my former life out of this. You know where I'm coming from and we both know what we've decided to do with our lives together.

Pause

So tell me, how are you going to handle it? What are you going to tell her?

Kevin What do you want to know for? I mean, it's no real concern of yours is it?

Kitty You are my concern now, Kevin, and what affects your life also affects mine. (*Going to him*) I want to help you. You must have thought about it. Let's talk it through; I don't want to put words in your mouth, but I don't want you weakening. If your wife has any sense she'll try to talk you out of it. A few well-chosen words from me will help your resolve. I don't want to lose you now. Now that we've decided it's for the best for us.

Kevin (*sighing*) Yes, you're right. As usual. You always find the right things to say. That's one of the things I love about you. You're strong when it comes to the crunch. I should have met you years ago.

Kitty Time doesn't matter. When you feel like we do it's like forever. There is no clock in the soul, you know.

Kevin You say the most beautiful things.

They kiss

Kitty (*breaking off*) Hey, you've spoilt my make-up. I spent an age putting it on. (*She goes to the mirror*) Oh, look what you've done. I shall have to touch it up again. You naughty boy!

Kevin (*laughing*) And may all your problems be small ones.
Kitty It's not a small problem. I want to look my best all the time. No more kissing, OK. That's your ration for tonight. And do get dressed, darling.
Kevin More like a six course meal, I'd say.
Kitty (*stopping*) You can be quite crude at times. You know that, don't you?
Kevin That's all part of the fun.
Kitty Fun?! For you maybe. For a gentlewoman like myself a more refined way of life is what I have come to expect.
Kevin Kitty! Just a bit of a joke. You should be used to my little ways by now.
Kitty Yes, well, I am I suppose. But just keep it down. Besides, you were going to tell me about the tragic leaving scene with your wife.
Kevin Oh, that's rich. You wipe away the nine years of my married life in a sentence, as (*he begins to get dressed*) if it didn't mean a thing.
Kitty It doesn't to you, and especially to me. Now, darling, simply tell me what you are going to say. I want to know.
Kevin If you insist.
Kitty I do.
Kevin Then I shall tell her... I shall tell her...

Pause

Kitty Well...

Pause

Kevin Christ, do we have to?
Kitty I'm waiting.

Pause

Kevin I ...I ... shall ... tell her——
Kitty (*interrupting*) The truth. That you don't love her anymore. That you've met someone who you wish to spend the rest of your life with, who you do love and will go on loving. That it is useless to continue

in a marriage that has become empty and futile. That the future will be a far happier place for us all. That you — your wife, that is — will find someone else who, hopefully, will really love you and appreciate you for the warm, kind person you are. There, that wasn't so difficult after all was it?!

Kevin It's all right for you to stand there and say that. You won't be there. You won't see the look of hurt and betrayal on her face. What about the kids? You never mentioned the kids. I am their father, you know. I do still love them.

Kitty (*quietly*) They won't die because you leave. You will be able to see them; they're your children and I would expect a loving father to want to see them. I shan't stand in your way.

Kevin You'll see them too, with me?

Kitty Oh, I'm sure we can come to some happy arrangement, Kevin, for your children's sake.

Kevin Oh, Kitty, you're an angel. (*He goes to embrace her*)

Kitty Ah, Ah. Watch my make-up, mind.

They embrace

Now, tonight. You will tell her tonight?

Kevin (*breaking away*) Yes, yes. No. Jesus! I don't know.

Kitty (*taking hold of him*) You must. You promised. I can't go on another night like this. We've been through this over and over again. I will not be your "other woman" anymore. Kevin, it's ultimatum time. It's her or me; now, are you going to tell her? (*She moves her body against his*)

Kevin I'll tell her.

Kitty Tonight?

Kevin Tonight, you crazy bitch, tonight.

He flings her on the bed and kisses her hungrily. Her hand flaps protesting, then gives up

Kitty You are a bad boy. But I love you for it. What time is it?

Kevin (*looking at his watch*) Gone one.

Kitty Shit, is that the time! (*She jumps off the bed, goes to fix her make-up*)

Kevin Kitty, anyone would think you were going out.
Kitty I am.
Kevin What, at this hour?! Who with for Christ's sake?
Kitty Keep your beard on. It's only the nightclub under the service flats; we've been there together lots of times. You know all the faces and the suits. They're nice people, you know that.
Kevin I'm gobsmacked. I can't believe you. You want me to go home and tell my wife I'm leaving her when the person I'm leaving her for is off out nightclubbing.
Kitty Oh, Kevin, you're not going to be a meanie about this are you? There's no harm in it. I've arranged to meet Freda and Di. It's all perfectly innocent. If there was anything untoward I wouldn't have told you, would I? You do trust me don't you? And I am a big grown-up girl, honest. Tell me you trust me. Look, I'm not going to be long. Give me a ring later and tell me what's happened. And from now on I'm going to be extra-special nice to my little Kev. Just you wait and see. (*She moves her body and kisses him*) It's all right, isn't it?
Kevin Yes, I guess so. I've never met anyone who could wrap me around like this.
Kitty (*aside*) If only you knew.
Kevin What was that?
Kitty Nothing — just counting my blessings. Now, you must go, it's getting so late. (*She puts on her stole*) How do I look?
Kevin I could eat you.
Kitty You just did. Now, tell me how I look?
Kevin Terrific. OK, you're right, I'd better go and do the dirty deed.
Kitty My brave man.
Kevin I'll leave my briefcase and coat here; no need to take them tonight.
Kitty (*slyly*) I'd prefer it if you took them. Later you can leave them, later. You know how tidy I like the place to be. A real fetish with me, I'm afraid. (*She kisses him*)
Kevin I'll ring as soon as I can. You will be back won't you?
Kitty Cross my heart and hope to ...
Kevin Hope to what?
Kitty Die if I don't.
Kevin You're lovely! (*He takes her to the door*)

Kitty Yes, it has been said before. Come on, let me take you to the lift. Give the other residents something else to talk about.
Kevin Something else?
Kitty Us, silly. Oh, don't forget this. (*She hands him his briefcase*)
Kevin Kitty, I don't want to.
Kitty Kevin, you must go. Now. Come on, soonest done, soonest over, eh, love. (*She leads him off*)

Kevin and Kitty exit

The Lights go out in Kitty's bedroom and come up on Kevin and Frances's bedroom

Frances enters and begins to take her make-up off, leading to...

Scene 2

Frances (*looking at a watch on the dressing table*) Kevin's late.

Pause

Later than usual, anyway.

Pause

He's probably got held up somewhere.

Pause

Yes, that's it. Entertaining some client or other I expect. Still, good luck to him I say. Doing well in his job. Promotion after promotion. Never thought he'd make managing director though. Not that I'd say anything against him mind. I just didn't think he had it in him.

Pause

(*Small laugh*) When I think back how uncouth he was when we first met at university. Both in our final year we were. Him all acne and bony limbs. Me all shy and flustered, even after three years. It's not that I led a sheltered life. Well, I suppose I did really. It was my parents. Always there to take me there and pick me up at the end of term. Boys soon got the message: stay away! My father hung a sign on me that said "Visitors forbidden". Oh, some tried, but it was too inbuilt. The fear, the anxiety of that first date showed up so much they never bothered again. No-one bothered again. After a while. In the end I led just as sheltered a life there as I had done at home. Not that I minded. I'd hear the other girls talk of copulating like shaking hands. Not for me, I said. If it's that important for them to want it so bad, I'll keep it for someone worthwile.

So there I was, twenty-one, never been kissed, kicked or screwed. A real proper virgin. Kevin was just the same. No-one had looked at him either. He was worse than me. Ever so ignorant. (*She laughs*) We used to think you did it in your belly button. Well, we found out didn't we. Sooner rather than later, thank God. Kevin's best friend lent him a book—The *Joy of Sex* I think it was. We soon made up for lost time. I was on the pill by then, so it was quite safe. My parents never knew, of course. I'd got into the habit of deceiving them at an early age. Lies never hurt as long as you're not found out. And they never did.

They approved of Kevin straight away, with his short hair and hand-knitted jumpers. "There's a dependable young man if ever I saw one", my father told me one day. My friends, such as I had, were always telling me too. Marry Kevin, they said. He'll be such a good, safe and dependable husband. They were right too. He was. He is. I wanted us to live together, but my parents and, strangely, Kevin, wouldn't hear of it. "You marry with our blessing or nothing." I can hear my father now.

It wasn't I was against marriage, but I began to question what did I want out of life. I've never been a rebel, but I'd never seen the grass on the other side of the fence. By the time I did it was too late.

Pause

(*Quietly*) Tom, our first child, is not Kevin's. No, I didn't mean to be unfaithful. It just sort of happened that way. Kevin was away on company business for a few days over a weekend. We had been trying for a baby for a few months with no show. I belonged to the local campanologists and went to practice every Friday. They didn't usually go for a drink, but it was someone's birthday so, as Kevin was away, I went and this chap gave me a lift home. One thing led to another and... (*She stops*) The father doesn't know and Kevin never suspected Tom wasn't his child. But I know and I carry the guilt. It wasn't any different with someone else. I can't even remember what it was like.

I'm not a feminist. Me, I like wearing a bra; the size of my tits I don't have much choice. I like to think back to before I had my two children. I thought a lot in those good old days. To me one of the great mysteries of life used to be what do people think about when they're putting on their knickers first thing in the morning. Then one morning I woke up and realized. Nothing. Just a big Z. Zilch. The thought quite terrified me. I suppose I got what I wanted out of life. A nice, safe, comfortable existence. Now—I'll never know.

The door is heard to go, R

That'll be Kevin. (*She returns to her make-up*)

Kevin comes in holding a glass

Leading to...

Scene 3

Frances Hello, darling. Had a good evening?
Kevin (*standing shamefacedly*) Got myself a drop of scotch.
Frances (*busy taking make-up off*) So I see. You'll want to watch your liver — you know how much hard liquor upsets you.
Kevin Just the one, darling. No harm in that.
Frances (*sniffing*) You smell smoky again. Your clothes reek of tobacco.
Kevin Really, I hadn't noticed.
Frances I suppose it's the golf club bar — always so smoky in there. Take your clothes off and I'll take them to the cleaners to get rid of the smell.

Kevin stands sheepishly

Well, what are you waiting for — a starting pistol?

Pause

Kevin You're up late.
Frances Thought I'd wait up for you. Have a chat.
Kevin Good. Kids OK?
Frances Fine. Tom got a new teacher in his class today. Doesn't know if he likes her. Says she smells of old books. Not that he knows what old books smell like. Sharon wet herself at nursery school. I think we'll have to change the one she goes to. St Paul's is highly recommended, but there's a long waiting list and I don't know if we can ...
Kevin (*interrupting*) I've got something to say to you ...
Frances Oh, yes. I've heard that tone of voice before. Sounds like you've been drinking.
Kevin No I haven't.
Frances Well, your voice always takes on that semi-serious sound when

you get maudlin. Drives me to distraction. Does this mean we're in for one of your heart-to-hearts?

Kevin What do you mean?

Frances You know. You do this from time to time. How you feel about the job. Where you fit in. Where I fit in. The children, worries. I'll listen. But if I fall asleep halfway through don't be upset. I'm dead tired from looking after your numero uno son and one and only daughter all day.

Kevin (*pause*) This will come as a shock to you, but I've got someone else.

Frances Really. Nice is she? (*She is sorting out children's clothes from a basket*)

Kevin Is that all you've got to say?

Frances So, you're having it off with someone else. Fine. OK by me.

Kevin Look. I'm serious.

Frances OK. You're seriously having it off with someone else. Good. I'm glad. It's about time you had a bit of fun. God knows, you can't expect it from me. I'm too knackered to bother about that.

Kevin I don't think you understand. I'm in love with her.

Frances You'll get over it.

Kevin I don't want to get over it. I want her.

Frances So, have her.

Kevin You are not taking me seriously.

Frances You cannot be serious. How do you expect me to take you seriously? OK, you've had a bit of a fling. I'm a modern wife. I can take this on board. But if you think some jumped-up little madam is going to queer our nest you've got another thing coming. Besides, we've got my parents' ruby wedding coming up — you wouldn't want to spoil that would you?

Kevin (*after a pause*) She said you'd be difficult.

Frances Kevin, I am not being difficult. I am being realistic. You going off with some fly-by-night is part of your dreams maybe. Part of your fantasy. But it is not part of our real lives, believe me.

Kevin She is not a fly-by-night.

Frances Oh, yes. Society hostess I'll bet. Out of the Anita Roddick role model. Life career woman, go-getter choosing our little Kevin as the man behind the throne is she?

Kevin No.
Frances I thought not. (*Pause*) Well, tell me about her.
Kevin Why do you want to know?
Frances If I've been half sharing your appendage with another woman I feel I have a right to know what she is.
Kevin She is not a "she". She is the woman who ...
Frances Who what?
Kevin Who shows me a helluva lot more understanding than you do.
Frances Ah. Listens to you does she? And I don't.
Kevin It's not like that.
Frances Tell me about it.
Kevin You are determined not to let this faze you.
Frances Look, I've known you for ten years. How do you expect me to take this? Lying down. No! Don't answer that! (*She laughs*)
Kevin Will you take me seriously?
Frances No!
Kevin Why not?
Frances You're just too ridiculous for words. (*Pause*) OK, you want to talk about it. Go on.

Pause

Kevin I don't know what to say. What do you want to know?
Frances Tell me about this wonderful woman who's swept you off your feet. What does she do?
Kevin Do?
Frances Give me credit for some intelligence. I take it she's single. God forbid she can't be married. So she must have some way of earning a living. Yes?
Kevin Yes.
Frances Well, what?
Kevin She's a hostess at the golf club.
Frances A what?
Kevin A hostess. She sees to people who come in. Important people.
Frances And what does she do when she's not "seeing to" people? This vastly career orientated existence can't take up all of her time.
Kevin She works behind the bar. But only when called upon to do so.

Frances A barmaid!

Kevin No. Not all of the time.

Frances (*laughing*) And I thought you were serious.

Kevin I am. It's been going on for some time.

Frances How long?

Kevin Nearly two years. I've got to know her pretty well.

Frances Not enough.

Kevin She says there is no clock in ...

Frances I don't care what she says. To know someone, Kevin, to really know someone, you have to live with them. Day in, day out. I mean is she aware of your wind problem?

Kevin (*tiredly*) Let's not start that.

Frances Don't tell me you've been keeping it back from her. Holding it back until you got home. Saving it all up for us were you?

Kevin That's unfair.

Frances Hah! You certainly bring the worst out in yourself, if you'll pardon the pun. I'll never forget the time we were making love and there, right in the middle of the climax, you let out a great big rasping fart. Well, that certainly killed any climax for me for the next few times. Scared you'd do it again. I didn't give you baked beans for weeks just in case.

Kevin I'm glad you brought that up.

Frances What?

Kevin Sex.

Frances Oh, not been getting enough conjugal rights have we? Turned to someone else in desperation? Getting your oats as forbidden fruit ...

Kevin She's not like that. It's wonderful with her.

Frances You poor, misguided fool. (*Pause*) Don't you know what it's all about. Listen, a long time ago I came to realize it doesn't matter. Sex. It's different for you. I know sex drives a man far greater than it would ever do me. The thing is, Kevin, why it doesn't matter. I can change from you and you to different people but, at the end of the day, we're doing the same thing. You've obviously got bored with me sexually; in ten years time you'll get bored with her, sexually. So it doesn't matter who you end up with sexually 'cos, in the end, you end up totally bored out of your mind sexually anyway. So stay with me, hon. You've got everything to lose and nothing to gain if you go.

Kevin I can't accept that. You think that, not me.

Frances Oh, Kevin. In years to come you'll know that. Why not accept it now. You'll save yourself a lot of heartbreak and grief if you do.

Kevin It sounds like you're taking me seriously at last.

Frances No, Kevin. I'm taking myself seriously, not you. If you are saying to me that some strumpet of a barmaid has got her hooks into you and thinks she can make it permanent, you have got another thing coming. You have a devoted wife, two lovely children, and a home you can be proud of. If all you are bothered about is a piece of skin, then you can have that from now until death from me. And that *is* serious. (*Pause*) Well?

Kevin I can't. My mind is made up. You've had your say. Let me have mine.

Frances goes to interrupt

No, don't interrupt. I believe in her. She means more to me than what we've ever done. I hear what you say, but it's no good. I can't hack this. I want out of this. I think you're the most loving mother our kids could ever have, but there's no way I see me any more in your life.

Frances You really mean it. In spite of all I've said, you mean to do it.

Kevin She knows I mean it. She wants me and she bloody well takes me seriously even if you don't!

Frances That's because she wants your money, Kevin. Not what you stand for.

Kevin No. She loves me for what I am.

Frances (*after a pause*) Then damn you, Kevin Hargreaves. Damn you to hell. (*She stands and begins to pack a suitcase*)

Kevin What are you doing?

Frances What does it look like? Packing. (*Pause*) I'll take the kids and go to my mother's. You can stay here and suffer the humiliation of the loss of your wife and children.

Kevin Now, hold on.

Frances The time for "holding on" is gone. I could have put up with your affair. We could have lived quite happily knowing you were coming back to be a father. Now you've had it. I don't suppose you've even thought about HIV in these liberated times? Let me warn you, Kevin, don't you ever come near me or my kids again. (*She hits him on the face*)

Frances goes to get the children up and dressed. Ad lib off stage conversation. She comes back

She picks up the suitcase

Give me the car keys.

Kevin does so

You know, I was really looking forward to growing old with you. That's how much I loved you. Now I'm going to take you for every fucking penny you've got in the fucking bank.

She turns on her heel and goes

Slam of door

Leading to ...

Scene 4

Kevin (*standing looking off*) Well, I guess that's what you wanted, old son. No more wife. Kids gone, too. Peace at last. No more nagging from her. (*He sits on the bed*) Great! (*He listens*) My God, but it's quiet. Still, be better when I'm living with Kitty. Funny, Fran never asked her name. Oh, well. I suppose she'll find out soon enough.

This will shock 'em down at the golf club. My God — I hope they don't withdraw my membership! Suppose they gave Kitty the push?! No, they wouldn't do that. Would they? They're a very straitlaced lot down there. Still, we'll still have one another. To the end, she said. Somehow, I believe that more than marriage vows. There's a lot more meaning to words when you say them in bed. Perhaps the marriage service should take place in bed. Right after making love. Have to get the timing right, of course. But relationships might mean more!

Christ, what about Fran's folks? The ruby wedding coming up. I can just hear the conversation. "That Kevin's a right bastard. I always knew he'd turn out to be a wrong one. " This from Fran's dad. Her mother, simpering as usual, agreeing with him, as usual, saying "well, he did seem a nice boy all those years ago." "Oh, come on, Mum, you could see it in his eyes. He wasn't Church, like our family. No faith, no moral fibre in his backbone. He had to go wrong eventually." Jesus, they always made me sick with their pious condemnation of all things different. Well, they've certainly got something different now. *(Pause)*

My mates will understand, naturally. Got yourself a nice bit of stuff at last. Better than Fran, eh! Nudge, nudge. Wink, wink. Say no more. *(Pause)*

Apart from Jeff, my best friend. He won't understand at all. He liked Fran. I suppose it was from when they did that bell ringing all those years ago. Couldn't stand it myself; never got involved. That's it really, I've never got involved at all. One of life's onlookers I classified myself as. Or rather, that's how life cast my part in life. No-one ever thought of asking me to do this or that.

I was always the one left out at the end of the evening on my own. Whereas others would go canoodling with girls, or at least be invited back for coffee. I always ended up walking home, on my own. Until I met Fran. Then life had a purpose, a meaning I hadn't had before. People began inviting me —us — to parties, events, functions. I suppose it was because we were a couple. The world caters for couples. It endures single people as long as they keep quiet. Make a fuss as a couple and you are a force; things get done for you; others react — two people mean trouble. One person can be ignored or shouted down. So we met and we married. I got a job, lowly paid, but with prospects. I didn't know then what I wanted from life. You never do that young. So I worked hard, long hours, training, exams, time away from home. Missing Fran. I loved her then. Part of her anyway. We had kids. The job got better. I worked my way up. Always conforming to what people expected. To what people demanded. Yes sir, no sir, anything you want, sir. Yes, Fran. No, Fran. The baby wants a new pushchair, right away, Fran. I acquiesced to it all because I had to; to survive in this stinking, lousy world.

People thought the world of me. Why not? I'd done nothing to displease them. I never did. Until, one day I made it to the top of the pile— managing director, a lovely wife and two smashing kids. The world was suddenly my oyster after years of struggle. It was then I thought "Fuck it", I'm going to do something for me.

I was entertaining clients quite a lot, virtually every night until late. When I got home Fran, being tired, was usually asleep, snoring away. It always amazed me how someone so seemingly lovely could snore like an Irish navvy after sixteen pints of Guinness. Sometimes she'd rattle the window panes. I would be there listening to this sometimes until the dawn chorus came up; in the morning she would get up and say "Hello dear, did you sleep well?" I didn't have the heart to tell her.

Kitty happened, as these things do, quite by accident. I was supposed to be away on a business trip which was cancelled at the last minute. Taking solace at the golf club with some friends early in the evening, I realized I hadn't told Fran. Kitty was behind the bar and being pestered by the club rake. I stepped in and made things all right. At the end of the evening I offered her a lift home and one thing led to another. Only they didn't end there. I stayed the night. Then another. I suppose I am a bastard for doing that. I wanted sex and I got what I wanted. For the first time in my life I was doing something for me.

I get a hard-on just thinking about her and what she does to me. It was never like that with Fran. That's why I can't agree with her. It is different and better. Kitty keeps mentioning the better things to come. I think sometimes she's a little kinky, though we've never tried anything like that. Not yet, anyway.

Well, if that's what she likes then that's OK with me. I'm fed up with the normal everyday grind. Fran used to say to me when I was starting a bit of foreplay "and don't stick your tongue in my mouth". So I stopped. Kitty loves me I know that. I can depend on her. No kids for us. There'll be just the two of us — forever.

Kitty walks into her bedroom

Both lights are now on and Kitty dials the telephone during Kevin's final speech. Leading to...

Scene 5

Kevin (*picking up the telephone*) Hello... Kitty? You took a chance ringing up. You don't even know what's happened.
Kitty If your wife had answered I'd have put the phone down. So tell me. What did happen?
Kevin She's gone. And she's taken the kids with her.
Kitty What did you say?
Kevin You should have heard me, I was great!
Kitty I bet. Gone where?
Kevin To her mum's.
Kitty That's great!
Kevin Yes! That means you can sell your flat and move in here.
Kitty (*taken aback*) Oh, no. I hadn't planned on that at all.
Kevin Why not? You've got nothing to keep you there, not now, and it will be so much more comfortable for you here.
Kitty Well, yes. But this is my home. I have all my things here. Much better for you to move in here. I'm all kitted out for you. Besides, how could I move in there. You would expect your wife to appear round each corner. Instead you'd see me. No, there's too many memories of your wife and children there. Much nicer for you to come here.
Kevin But this is where I live. I thought that you would want ...
Kitty Kevin, you're mine now. You do as I say or there'll be trouble.
Kevin That's what I like about you. You're so forceful.

Kitty You don't know the half of it yet. Just wait 'til I get you alone now I know you're mine. What did you say to her?

Kevin It was very difficult actually. I laid down the law about what was what. She argued, cried, and then saw there was no chance and left without a word!

Kitty I always knew you'd be masterful when it came to it.

Kevin Well, you know what they say: when the going gets tough, the tough get going.

Kitty Words that are music to my heart, Kevin. Oh, I've got you something interesting to wear. I simply know you'll love it, darling. Will drive you wild with desire when you see what my outfit is to match.

Kevin When can we meet again. Can I come round now?

Kitty Er, it is late and I must get my beauty sleep you know. You do want me at my best the first time with "us".

Kevin Yes, you're absolutely right. I'm feeling pretty bushed after all of tonight's traumas.

Kitty's doorbell goes

What's that? Sounds like your front doorbell.

Kitty Oh, nothing, darling. I expect it's the early delivery, milk or something. These service flats have funny hours. I'll ring you first thing in the morning, OK darling?

Kevin If you say so. 'Til then, sleep well, love.

Kitty You too. 'Bye for now. Love you. (*She blows a kiss into the phone*)

Kitty puts her phone down. Kevin cradles his, kisses it and puts it down

Kevin exits

Kitty's front doorbell goes again

Kitty exits

Muffled conversation heard off

Leading to...

SCENE 6

Kitty (*off*) It's in there. Take as long as you like getting ready, love.

Kitty comes back on

She looks at the phone. She laughs quietly at first, then out loud

> Got you, you bastard. Got you by the short and curlies. A man of my own. To keep for my own. One who's going to keep me more in the comfort I should be in. Oh, Kevin, you lovely man. What fun I will have with you now. (*She claps her hands, goes to look in the mirror*) God, you look like shit. Urgent repairs are called for I think. Don't want any complaints, do we. Got to keep the customer satisfied. (*She makes up some more*) Oh dear; takes longer now, babes, doesn't it?

Pause

> (*Smiling*) You have done well for yourself, haven't you. Two years ago you were on your beam ends, slagging off police sergeants for getting too nosey in your affairs. Mind you, they didn't mind a look underneath, the dirty sods. Nor a feel either. (*She shudders*) The law is a law unto itself.

Pause

> Lucky though, getting that job at the golf club. I was just what they needed. Still, all I had to do was smile as the drunk men leered and tried to touch me up. I could hack all that after what I'd been through. Now I've got it made. Just what I wanted. A flat, all found, no ties and the best clothes to wear. Just by using a bit of noddle. That's what Mum said I should do right from the start. Even at six years old.

Poor Mum, bless your heart, you certainly had it tough. That useless father of ours running off when he did. There we were, the two of us, destitute, abandoned, not a penny in the world. Dirty council flats maybe, but you kept us together somehow. Jumble sale clothes on our backs and fish fingers for lunch, dinner and tea. We survived. "Kitty," she said "make something of yourself. Make'em pay, Kitty, for all this, make'em pay." God, what a handle you gave me, Mum. Kitty. Just because she bought me that damned kitten and I never stopped saying "Here kitty, kitty" for six whole months. The kitten died but the name stuck with me. Poor Mum. God rest her soul. She died of leukaemia when I was sixteen. She'd taught me all she knew by then. How to use men. To get them to provide with no strings attached. I remember many the time I put her to bed drunk with the occasional bruise on her face. But we survived. I survived. You needn't have worried, Mother, I've done well all right, better than you. *(Breath)* But that's what you intended all along isn't it?

Sometimes it shows. Oh, I've seen other women looking at me and I think: I know what you're thinking. You're that tart, aren't you? Well, keep your hands off my fella or I'll tear your eyes out. I can see it in their eyes. The fear, the jealousy, the hatred. That's why Kevin was such a godsend. He never brought his wife along to the club. It was easy to flirt with him, entice him, and then once I'd touched him he didn't stand a chance. Poor wife, poor Kevin, *(with a smile)* lucky Kitty.

A noise off

All right, luv, Mummy's coming to see you now. Is Momma's boy ready for his medicine?

She goes out

Black-out

Scene 7

The same. Several weeks later

Kevin comes in with his briefcase and goes to stand looking in the mirror. Kitty comes on

Kitty You're late. I can't be having you coming in here late. You'd better get your gear on. I'm in the mood for a good long one tonight. Don't just stand there; get on with it or I'll teach you a real lesson. (*She sniffs*) You've not farted again, have you? God, I'll have to get the aerosol out. I can't stand the smell of that either. Come on, Kevin, join in, it's what you wanted after all.

Kitty exits

Kevin goes to sit on the bed. He sobs quietly then more loudly

Kevin You fool. You big bloody fool. Did you really want this? Was this the forever you planned together? Fran was right. The end is only the end if it's worth it. Now Fran is divorcing me. I feel so trapped, there's nowhere to go. I can't go back to Frances and no-one wants to know me any more. My friends ignore me. I walk down a corridor at work and I can hear people sniggering behind my back. It's so undeserving. My best mate says I've gone soft in the head, and for what? Loving someone else? I just don't understand. Maybe if I made it all legal they would understand. Life's too short to go on like this. I feel more sinned against than sinning. I feel sometimes that I'm in a bad dream and I'll wake up, find that Fran is still there, the kids are in bed and that Kitty was just a figment of my imagination. But no matter how hard I pinch myself, I never seem to be able to wake up...

Kitty enters wearing a dressing-gown

Kitty What, not ready yet? Really, you are being a naughty boy tonight.
Kevin Kitty, we must talk.
Kitty Oh, hello. Found your voice at last have you?

Kevin Kitty, why don't we plan to get married?
Kitty What on earth for?
Kevin It would make things better if our intentions were out in the open.
Kitty Are you talking about what people think? I don't give a toss what people think and neither should you.
Kevin People are saying things behind my back.
Kitty Cut it, Kevin! You know, I sometimes wonder if you've got all your chairs round the table.
Kevin I thought that's what you would want. Christ, I know we never talked about it before, but it's the logical conclusion, isn't it? Oh, I realize you don't want children. The way you detest other people's told me that.
Kitty Girls like me don't get married. Oh, don't look so shocked. I'm perfectly happy to go on as we are. I never wanted another man's name and I don't intend to start now.
Kevin I didn't leave my wife and kids for a life like this, God forbid.
Kitty But you did, and now you've got what you deserve, believe me. You're more locked into me mentally than you ever were with your wife. A marriage certificate would never give us that.
Kevin It would show the world we were serious.
Kitty Kevin Hargreaves, you're a pratt! Let me tell you the facts of life. (*She begins to undress him*) People don't get married any more to conform to some social more and be accepted. They did when you first got married, but times have changed and you will have to change too. There's no moral fibre left any more, you see. Couples shack up for a couple of years first 'cos they fancy one another. If someone else they fancy more comes along after a couple of years then they go off with them. It's a lot more simple than divorcing all the time and not half so costly.
Kevin You said it would be us forever.
Kitty No, Kevin, you said that, not me. I'll never say that.
Kevin Are you saying you'd leave me then if you did meet someone.
Kitty No, I'm not saying that either.
Kevin Then what? I want a future.
Kitty You are funny. Come here, let me tell you a story. (*She takes him and kneels him down at the end of the bed and holds him*) Are you sitting comfortably. Then I'll begin. When you were very, very little,

did you ever have an extra-special favourite toy?

Kevin Yes, I had a teddy bear...

Kitty You loved that teddy bear to distraction, I can tell. Kevin, we're grown up now and you are my extra-special favourite toy and I'll never leave you and never let you go. There, does that make you happy?

Kevin It's not exactly what I had in mind.

Kitty It doesn't matter what you had in mind, it's what you've got. As you make your bed...

Kevin No! (*He breaks away*) You can't do this to me.

Kitty It's showtime is it ...? Oh, yes I can. Now come here before I lose...

A chase ensues round the bedroom. Music begins to play more and more out of key. Strobe lighting. Kevin eventually ends up under the sheets and begins to shout out

Kitty exits and is replaced by Frances

Kevin No. No! Leave me alone, I can't stand it any more. Stop. Stop. Help me.

Frances Wake up, Kevin, wake up. You're screaming the house down. Come on, wake up.

Kevin Fran?

Frances Yes! It's all right, darling, you were having a nightmare and screaming out loud. Are you all right now?

Kevin Thank God. For one awful moment I thought ... Fran, are you OK?

Frances Yes, just a little shaken by being suddenly woken up so violently. You stay there, darling. I'll go and see if Tom and his sister are asleep. Back in a mo.

Frances exits

Kevin (*his head falls back. Sighing*) Now if only I could sleep...

The other bedroom door opens and into the light steps Kitty, carrying a whip in all her glory. She advances into the room

Kitty Right, Kevin Hargreaves.

Kevin jerks awake

Now your nightmare really begins.

She forces him out of bed and towers over him holding the whip, about to strike. A lighting effect of gobo with bars should then flash on, coupled with a cell door clanging shut. This is the final picture as we go to——

Black-out

CURTAIN

FURNITURE AND PROPERTY LIST

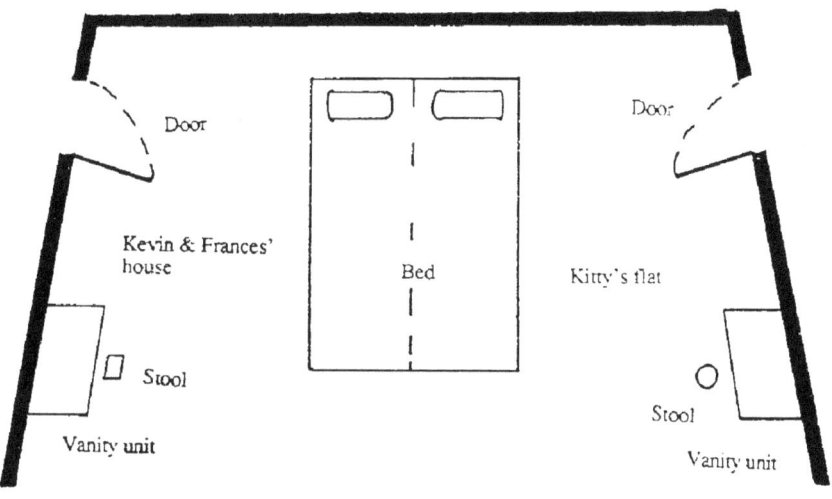

On stage: Bed
2 vanity units. *On one:* make-up, dressing. *On other:* watch, dressing
2 stools
Clothes basket (**Frances's** area)
Telephones L and R

Off stage: Cigarettes (**Kitty**)
Stole (**Kitty**)
Briefcase (**Kitty**)
Glass (**Kevin**)
Children's clothes (**Frances**)
Suitcase (**Frances**)
Dressing gown (**Kitty**)
Whip (**Kitty**)

Personal: **Kevin:** watch

LIGHTING PLOT

Property fittings required: nil

To open: General interior lighting

Cue 1   **Kevin** and **Kitty** exit   (Page 6)
Crossfade to **Kevin** *and* **Frances's** *bedroom*

Cue 2   **Kitty** walks into her bedroom   (Page 17)
Bring up lights R

Cue 3   **Kitty** goes out   (Page 20)
Black-out. When ready, bring up lights R

Cue 4   Music begins to play   (Page 23)
Strobe lighting. Cut when **Kitty** *exits*
Revert to previous lighting

Cue 5   **Kitty** towers over **Kevin**   (Page 24)
Gobo effect of prison bars

EFFECTS PLOT

Cue 1	**Frances:** "... I'll never know" *The door is heard* R	(Page 8)
Cue 2	**Frances** goes *Slam of door*	(Page 14)
Cue 3	As Lights change for Scene 5 *Telephone*	(Page 17)
Cue 4	**Kevin** " ... all of tonight's traumas" **Kitty's** *doorbell rings*	(Page 18)
Cue 5	**Kevin** exits *Doorbell*	(Page 18)
Cue 6	A chase ensues round the bedroom *Music, playing more and more out of key*	(Page 23)
Cue 7	As gobo effect flashes on *Sound of cell door clanging shut*	(Page 24)

www.ingramcontent.com/pod-product-compliance
Lightning Source LLC
Chambersburg PA
CBHW070455050426
42450CB00012B/3284